Sports Strategies

TENNIS STRATEGIES

BY DAVID J. CLARKE

SportsZone
An Imprint of Abdo Publishing
abdobooks.com

abdobooks.com

Published by Abdo Publishing, a division of ABDO, PO Box 398166, Minneapolis, Minnesota 55439.

Printed in the United States of America, North Mankato, Minnesota.
102023
012024

THIS BOOK CONTAINS RECYCLED MATERIALS

Cover Photo: Mine Kasapoglu/Anadolu Agency/Getty Images
Interior Photos: Clive Brunskill/Getty Images Sport/Getty Images, 5, 19, 29; Leon Neal/AFP/Getty Images, 6–7; Red Line Editorial, 8; Michael Dodge/Getty Images Sport/Getty Images, 10; Ian Walton/Getty Images Sport/Getty Images, 13; Daniel Pockett/Getty Images Sport/Getty Images, 14–15; Martin Keep/AFP/Getty Images, 16–17; Central Press/Hulton Archive/Getty Images, 20; Cameron Spencer/Getty Images Sport/Getty Images, 22–23; Koichi Kamoshida/Getty Images Sport/Getty Images, 25; Leon Neal/Getty Images Sport/Getty Images, 26–27; Simon Bruty/Anychance/Getty Images Sport/Getty Images, 30–31, 36; Fox Photos/Keystone/Hulton Archive/Getty Images, 33; Trevor Jones/Allsport/Hulton Archive/Getty Images, 35; Justin Setterfield/Getty Images Sport/Getty Images, 38–39; Pierre Gleizes/AP Images, 41; Minas Panagiotakis/Getty Images Sport/Getty Images, 42–43; Adam Pretty/Getty Images Sport/Getty Images, 45

Editor: Steph Giedd
Series Designer: Joshua Olson

Library of Congress Control Number: 2023939421

Publisher's Cataloging-in-Publication Data

Names: Clarke, David J., author.
Title: Tennis strategies / by David J. Clarke
Description: Minneapolis, Minnesota: Abdo Publishing, 2024 | Series: Sports strategies | Includes online resources and index.
Identifiers: ISBN 9781098292485 (lib. bdg.) | ISBN 9798384910428 (ebook)
Subjects: LCSH: Sports teams--Juvenile literature. | Teamwork (Sports)--Juvenile literature. | Athletes--Training of--Juvenile literature. | Tennis--Juvenile literature.
Classification: DDC 796.01--dc23

TABLE OF CONTENTS

INTRODUCTION

Tennis is a sport in which small moments can have a big impact. One mistake can cost a player a game. That game could then cost that player the set. So on every point, each player has to make smart decisions. And since tennis is played at such a fast pace, those choices must be made in a fraction of a second.

Sometimes a player chooses to attack an opponent with big shots. Some instead try to attack by getting to the net quickly. Others sit back and defend, keeping rallies going until the right moment arrives to hit a winning shot. And players with particularly strong serves might rely on that to dominate their matches.

Match strategy might change for certain players on different types of courts. And doubles tennis brings an entirely different element to the sport as the space for open shots becomes smaller. Each tennis match is a distinct clash of styles. And no matter where it is played and who is playing, exciting strategic battles play out every day on the court.

More than 23 million people play tennis in the United States, and there are approximately 1 billion tennis fans throughout the world.

cinch CHAMPIONSHIPS
BNP PARIBAS
Emirates FLY BETTER
ATP TOUR
NYETIMBER
oppo
Haier
cinch CHAMPIONSHIPS

Chapter 1

Serving and Returning

Court 18 at the All England Lawn Tennis Club does not usually feature the biggest matches at the annual Wimbledon Championships. But over three days in June 2010, it became the center of the tennis universe. That's because American John Isner and Frenchman Nicolas Mahut were locked in an epic match with no end in sight.

The two men had started the match at 6:13 p.m. on June 22. After completing four of five sets, the match was tied 2–2 when it was suspended due to darkness. It started again at 2:05 p.m. the next day. Isner and

John Isner delivers a serve to Nicolas Mahut at Wimbledon in 2010 during the longest match in Grand Slam history.

Mahut played for seven more hours before darkness suspended the match again. The players had already broken the record for the longest tennis match ever, but there was still no winner.

The reason was that neither could break the other's serve. The last service break for either player had come late in the second set. Both the third and fourth sets were won on tiebreakers after finishing 6–6. But since Wimbledon didn't use a tiebreaker rule in the fifth set at the time, one player had to break serve before the match could end.

Top Men's Serve Speeds

Here are 10 of the fastest servers in men's tennis history, based on their top recorded speed.

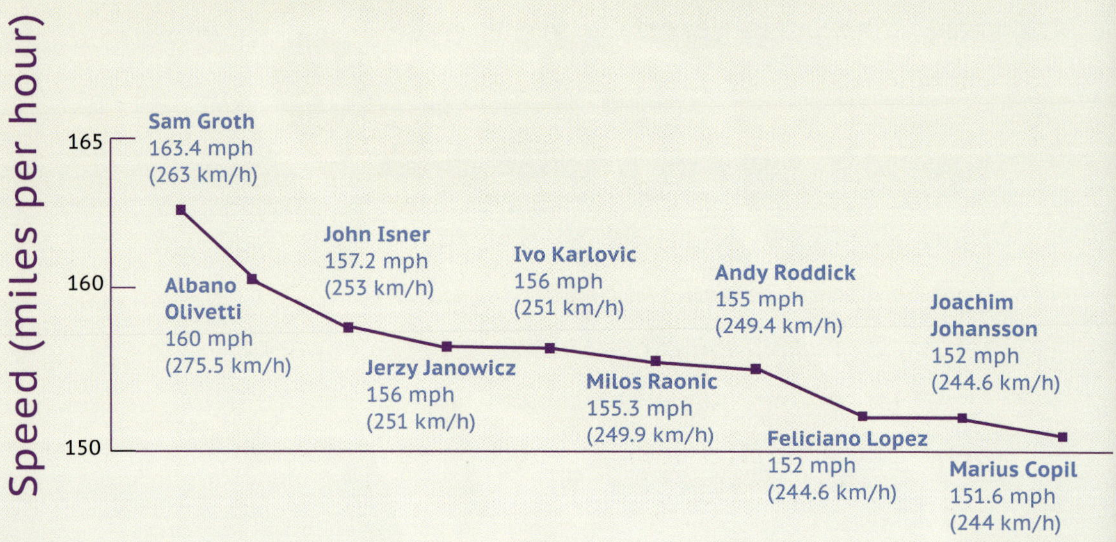

After about an hour of play on the third day, Isner had a chance. He led the fifth set 69–68. Mahut was serving at 30–30 but faulted on his first service attempt. He took speed off his second attempt. That allowed Isner to get a good forehand on the return. When Mahut returned that shot weakly, Isner unloaded a powerful forehand winner down the line.

That set up match point. This time, Mahut hit a hard serve to Isner's backhand. The American punched his return to the middle of the court. Mahut charged and tried a drop shot. But it went deeper than he had hoped. That allowed Isner to rip another winner down the line.

Isner collapsed on his back, both exhausted and elated. He then rose to hug Mahut at center court as the crowd gave both players an ovation. The fans were applauding the end of an 11-hour, five-minute match. But what they had also witnessed was just how important both serving and returning are to winning on the court.

POWER AND PLACEMENT

Tennis points can be played using a variety of strategies. But on every point, one player has to serve and the other has to return. This exchange can set the tone for an entire point.

When serving, many players are first trying to ace their opponent. Aces often look like big, powerful blasts when

Isner's fastest recorded serve was at the 2016 Davis Cup. It was 157.2 miles per hour (253 km/h).

professionals do it. And while aces are often hit powerfully, they also usually involve a lot of strategy. Servers try to always keep an opponent guessing. If the returner knows what's coming, it's easier to prepare. To avoid this, top players mix up their serves.

A player gets two attempts to serve on each point, so they usually take more risks on the first serve. On one, a player might hit a flat, powerful shot to one side of the service box. On the next, he or she might turn the racket to put spin on the ball. This might take speed off, but the spin will create a big bounce, or "kick," that is difficult to return.

Isner was recognized as one of the best servers ever to play men's tennis. Because of his 6-foot-10-inch frame, he hit the ball from a much higher angle than other players. That helped generate extra speed and also created huge kicks that returners had to deal with. In his career, Isner won just under 92 percent of his service games, one of the best percentages of all time.

JOHN ISNER: SERVICE ACE

John Isner is the all-time record holder in professional tennis with more than 14,000 aces in his career. He had 113 during his record-breaking 2010 Wimbledon match with Nicolas Mahut to set the single-match record.

THE SETUP

Not all players have Isner's powerful serve. After a 2022 match, top-ranked women's player Iga Świątek admitted she had to win points another way. Instead of going for aces, Świątek tries to set up the rest of the point by forcing her opponent to hit a weak return.

Players can do this in several ways. By hitting wide serves, they might force an opponent to lunge for a return. If the returner can't recover in time, that could open the court for a second-shot winner. A powerful serve to an opponent's backhand might be returned weakly. That allows the server to attack the ball coming forward, giving him or her a good chance at winning the point on the next shot.

A third type of serve is the body serve. This is hit directly at an opponent, forcing him or her to decide whether to hit a forehand or a backhand. Since that decision must come quickly, it can be difficult to get a good shot away. Again, that puts the server at an advantage for the rest of the point.

RETURN TO SENDER

The server starts every point with an advantage. The trick for the returner is to somehow take control of the point. The best way to do that is by hitting the ball deep or wide. But that is very difficult in the professional game. The average men's pro player serves 120 miles per hour (193 km/h). The average women's pro player serves 105 miles per hour (169 km/h). At those speeds, it's almost impossible to get a controlled shot on a return.

Most returns are defensive shots. The idea is just to keep the ball in play. But some players are better than others at returning the ball in a way that can help make the point more equal. Throughout his historic career, Rafael Nadal has been

Though Rafael Nadal started playing tennis at age four, his professional career began in 2001 as a 15-year-old junior competitor.

recognized as one of the best returners in professional tennis. One of his techniques is to stand as deep as he can. In many matches, Nadal sets up close to the back wall. That allows him more time to react to the serve as it comes in. It also gives him

the chance to load up a full swing and hit a more powerful return.

Standing that deep doesn't work for everyone. Because the player is so far back, there is more ground to cover on either side for serves that go up the center line or out wide. But Nadal's exceptional footwork and quickness allow him to take that chance. And through 2022, Nadal had won an amazing 42.4 percent of his return points. It's one of the reasons he entered the 2023 season with 22 major titles to his name.

Despite naturally being right-handed, Nadal plays his forehand with his left hand.

CHAPTER 2

ATTACKING THE NET

American Coco Gauff had just let a big chance slip away during the first set of the second round of the 2023 Australian Open. She had been up 3–1 against Emma Raducanu of England. But Gauff double-faulted to drop the next game. Now it was 3–2. Instead of cruising to a first-set victory, Gauff had to battle once again. She decided to get aggressive.

The players exchanged deep baseline shots on the first point of the next game. Finally, Gauff switched it up. She slowed her racket down and hit a feathery drop shot just

Coco Gauff pumps her fist after winning a point against Emma Raducanu at the 2023 Australian Open.

over the net. As Raducanu charged in, so did Gauff. By the time Raducanu reached the ball, the two players were about 10 feet (3 m) from each other. But Raducanu had spent a lot of energy sprinting forward from behind the baseline. She could only manage a backhand straight at Gauff. The American reacted quickly and popped a volley over Raducanu's head. Raducanu couldn't recover in time. The ball dropped into the backcourt and Gauff won the point.

Gauff went on to win that game and take control of the set once again. She eventually won it 6–3. Then she took the second set as well to move on to the third round. At age 18, Gauff was one of the hottest young stars in American women's tennis, and her willingness to attack the net was one reason why.

ANGLES

The more court that tennis players have available to shoot at, the better their chances are of winning a point. The best players can use their movement and foot skills to cut off their opponent's angles. One of the best ways to do this is by getting to the net. Once at the net, players can position themselves in such a way that almost every shot is right at them. Only perfect shots down the lines or expert lobs can make the net player move.

Gauff follows through on a backhand volley at the 2023 French Open.

Getting to the net is also a quick way to end points. When two professionals are at the baseline, they are both quick enough to get to almost every shot. That can lead to incredibly long rallies. Over the course of a three- or five-set match, all that running can wear down even the most fit player. By getting to the net quickly, a player can force the action a little more.

In 1971 Billie Jean King became the first female athlete to win at least $100,000 in yearly prize money.

SERVE AND VOLLEY

One of tennis's best-known tactics is the "serve and volley." To pull it off, a player tries to get to the net immediately after their serve. That way they can attack their opponent's return and put the point away quickly. In the 1960s, 1970s, and 1980s, legendary players such as Rod Laver, Billie Jean King, John McEnroe, and Martina Navratilova were known for their serve-and-volley skills. Among the four of them, they won 48 major singles titles.

However, all those players competed before modern racket and string technology changed tennis. In the modern game, players can get much more speed and topspin on their ground strokes. Since the ball is coming back much faster, there is less time to get to the net and cut off the angles.

Many players choose not to come to the net very often anymore. One study showed that female players at the 2002 Wimbledon tournament played about 800 serve-and-volley points. That number was down to fewer than 200 in 2018. Yet, the strategy still works. The same study showed that players won about 66 percent of the points when they tried the serve-and-volley strategy. Players are simply choosing not to do it as much. Gauff was a perfect example of this in her match against Raducanu. After volleying the winner in that crucial first-set game, Gauff stayed at the baseline for the rest of the game's points. But at a key moment in the match, she showed just how effective getting to the net can be.

The Chip and Charge

While "serve and volley" is the name used when a player is serving, the tactic has a different name when that player is the returner. Then it is called the "chip and charge." To pull it off, a returner will hit a sliced return to slow the ball down. They then use that extra time to charge the net.

Chapter 3

Playing the Baseline

Aryna Sabalenka of Belarus tossed the ball high and delivered a second serve. After unleashing the shot, she grimaced. It had gone long. The crowd at Rod Laver Arena in Melbourne, Australia, murmured at the double-fault. Sabalenka was leading Kazakhstan's Elena Rybakina 5–4 in the decisive third set of the 2023 Australian Open final. Before the missed serves, Sabalenka had led 40–30. But she had just double-faulted on championship point, sending the game to deuce.

Aryna Sabalenka follows through on a backhand during the 2023 Australian Open.

Some players might play it safe after that type of mistake, afraid to make another one. But Sabalenka quickly regrouped. She put Rybakina on the defensive with a big first serve to start the next point. Sabalenka then unloaded on the return ball. Her forehand exploded down the right sideline, landing in the corner, out of Rybakina's reach. The crowd cheered loudly after the perfect winner.

It wasn't surprising that Sabalenka had stayed aggressive. She had been playing that way the entire tournament and wasn't about to stop. Sabalenka ultimately won on her fourth championship point. After two weeks of powerful tennis, Sabalenka became the sport's brand-new major champion.

AGGRESSIVE BASELINERS

Modern tennis, both men's and women's, is mostly played at the baselines. Many rallies feature two players standing deep, exchanging ground strokes. Play doesn't stop until one of them either makes a mistake or hits a winner. However, though most players are standing back at the baseline, they aren't necessarily all playing the same way.

Changes in racket technology have affected the way tennis is played at the top level. Modern racket frames and strings produce more power and spin. Players today hit shots that were unheard of even 30 years ago. That has opened the door

Argentinian Juan Martín del Potro's aggressive baseline game helped him win his only Grand Slam title at the 2009 US Open.

for players who are known as aggressive baseliners, such as Sabalenka, to thrive.

The idea behind aggressive baseline play is fairly simple: stay deep, and try to make every shot difficult to return. That does not mean simply hitting the ball as hard as possible. Playing aggressive tennis also means trying to place shots down the lines or deep in the corners. While some players are happy just to keep a point going, aggressive players are trying to hit winners whenever possible. They like to move the ball from side to side on each shot as well. That way, even if their

opponent does return one, they will likely have to chase the next shot. Doing that on every point is difficult and tiring.

Playing this way is risky, however. Because these shots must be both precise and powerful, it is easy to make mistakes. Trying to hit shots so close to the lines runs a big risk of playing the ball wide or long. Aggressive players often make more unforced errors than more cautious players.

DEFENSIVE BASELINERS

The opposite of the aggressive baseliner is the defensive baseliner. These players also stay deep but tend to play safer shots. The idea is to keep a point going until they have a clear shot at a winner or until their opponent makes a mistake. Defensive baseliners don't force the action.

To play this way, a player needs to have great quickness. They must be able to cover the entire court and hit clean shots.

Novak Djokovic of Serbia plays a forehand during the Olympic Games in Tokyo, Japan, in 2021.

Defensive baseliners also tend to favor longer points. These players are usually the most physically fit athletes in the professional game.

At the 2023 French Open, Novak Djokovic won his 23rd Grand Slam singles title. No man has won more. And while Djokovic can play matches many ways, the Serbian's defensive skills are legendary. At the 2013 US Open final, Djokovic was up 3–2 on Rafael Nadal in the second set. Nadal was serving down 30–40. The two men then traded 54 shots in an amazing rally. Neither player moved off the baseline. But while Nadal was trying to finish off the point, Djokovic just kept putting the ball back in play with solid, clean shots.

Djokovic's final two shots in the rally showcased his defensive skills. After Nadal hit a hard backhand from one corner of the court to the other, Djokovic sprinted to reach it and return the ball.

The All-Court Player

A player who uses a variety of tactics in tennis is known as an all-court player. These players are comfortable playing as aggressive or defensive baseliners as well as coming to the net. Carlos Alcaraz of Spain is known as one of the better all-court players in the men's game today. He became the world's youngest year-end No. 1–ranked men's player after the 2022 season, when he was just 19.

Djokovic poses in front of the Eiffel Tower in Paris, France, with his 23rd Grand Slam trophy after winning the 2023 French Open men's singles title.

Nadal then tried to hit a hard shot the other way. But Djokovic recovered, sprinted back across the court, and played a backhand over the net. When Nadal's next shot went into the net, the epic point was over, and Djokovic had won the game.

Chapter 4

Different Surface, Different Game

Novak Djokovic stared across the net as his opponent, Italian Matteo Berrettini, readied to serve. Djokovic led the fourth set 5–3 at the 2021 Wimbledon men's final. It was also advantage Djokovic. With a 2–1 set lead, the Serbian was at championship point.

After Djokovic returned the serve, the two men settled into a baseline rally. They exchanged one-handed slicing backhands from corner to corner. Each time, the players had to handle

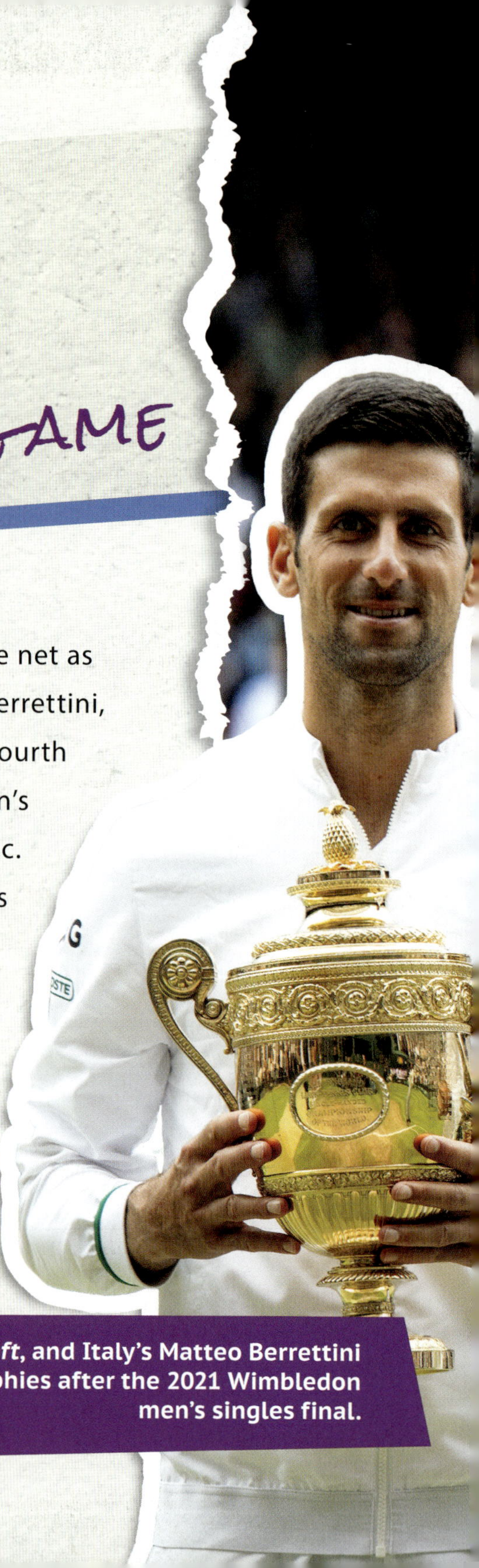

Serbia's Novak Djokovic, *left*, and Italy's Matteo Berrettini pose with the trophies after the 2021 Wimbledon men's singles final.

The Championships
Wimbledon
Runner-up
Gentlemen's Singles 2021

the speedy, low bounces off the slick grass surface at London's famous All England Club.

Finally, Berrettini's attempt came up too low. As the ball slammed into the net, Djokovic fell flat on his back to celebrate the victory. He had just tied the men's record for Grand Slam titles with 20. And three of them had come in 2021 alone. He had won on a hard court at the Australian Open. Djokovic then followed up by winning the French Open on a clay court. Now, in early July, he had conquered Wimbledon's grass.

MAKING ADJUSTMENTS

Professional tennis has four major tournaments. They make up what is known as the Grand Slam. The Australian Open is played first, in January. It's followed by the French Open in the spring. Wimbledon is contested in late June and early July. The US Open ends the major season in late August and early September. All four tournaments are difficult to win. And what makes it even more challenging is that they are played on three different surfaces.

Until 1978 all major tournaments were played on either grass or clay. In 1975 the US Open switched from grass to clay. Three years later, the tournament moved from clay to hard courts. The Australian Open made the change from grass to hard courts in 1988. Those changes made winning all four

John McEnroe of the United States plays on a hard court during the 1981 US Open.

very difficult. The style and strategy of tennis varies greatly depending on the surface. Players have to adapt their games to the unique conditions of each.

Hard courts are made of asphalt or concrete, which is covered by a substance called resin. The game tends to be very fast, and the bounces are high. But since the surface is smooth, there are few tricky bounces. Most tournaments are played on hard courts. Because of that, almost all professional players are capable of winning on the surface.

THE GRAND SLAM

Winning all four majors in one year is called the Grand Slam. Only five players have ever done it in singles play. However, only Steffi Graf of West Germany achieved the feat on grass, clay, and hard courts. Graf won all four majors in 1988. The other four players—Don Budge, Maureen Connolly, Rod Laver (twice), and Margaret Court—all won the Grand Slam when the Australian and US Open tournaments were still played on grass.

CLAY COURT SPECIALISTS

Clay courts offer players a different challenge. At the French Open, the red clay tends to slow the ball down when it bounces, and the ball still bounces high. Since players have more time to get to the ball, long points are more frequent. It's also more difficult for players to hit winners, so defensive players often do well on clay courts.

American Chris Evert was a dominant clay-court player during her career. From 1973 to 1979, she won 125 clay-court matches in a row. One of Evert's strengths was her ability to play defensively and get to the ball.

On the men's side, no player was ever better on clay than Rafael Nadal. The Spaniard's 14 French Open titles are seven more than any other player, male or female. Like Evert, Nadal is known for his ability to cover every inch of the court. And his

From 1973 to 1981, Chris Evert had a record of 189–1 in clay-court matches.

hard topspin shots are tough to handle, because the extra spin gives the ball even higher bounces.

Over the years, many players have been considered clay-court specialists. Though they never achieved legendary status in the sport, they thrived on clay. Austrian Thomas Muster won only one major title in his career, the 1995 French Open. But he was known as the "King of Clay" since 40 of his 44 tour titles came on the surface.

Roger Federer of Switzerland lines up a forehand at Wimbledon in 2021.

LAWN TENNIS

After tennis legend Roger Federer retired in 2022, the chairman of Wimbledon made sure to say that the Swiss great would be honored at the 2023 tournament. That was not a surprise. Over his dominant career, no men's player conquered the All England Club's tricky grass courts as Federer did. His record of eight championships included five straight from 2003 to 2007.

Only Martina Navratilova had more, with nine. Her first title was in 1978 and her last was in 1990.

Both Federer and Navratilova were great grass-court players for a few reasons. Unlike on clay and hard courts, the ball does not bounce high on grass. It skips and stays low. Players who close on the ball and hit it quickly after the bounce have more success. This is called taking the ball early. It was a strength of both players.

Federer and Navratilova also both served well. Points played on grass do not tend to last as long as those played on other surfaces. So getting the serve right is important. A good serve, even if it is not an ace, puts a player in position to win a point quickly. Wimbledon has always favored players who can play the serve-and-volley style. Navratilova is considered one of the best serve-and-volley players ever. Federer also played that style well, especially early in his career.

On grass, players need to be ready for anything. Over the course of a two-week tournament featuring several matches a day, the grass wears out, especially near the baseline. That means the ground is harder there, and the ball will bounce differently in the last few days of the tournament than in the first few. Couple that with the unpredictable bounces that already happen on grass, and it's a challenge for even the best players.

Chapter 5

Doubles Strategy

As Matthew Ebden lined up to take his serve, his partner, Max Purcell, crouched low in the middle of the court. The doubles team was tied at 4–4 in the fourth set of the 2022 Wimbledon men's final against Nikola Mektić and Mate Pavić. But Ebden and Purcell were trailing 2–1 in sets. This was a crucial game for the English duo.

It was advantage Ebden/Purcell, so one point would win the game. The duo made what happened next look easy. Ebden powered his serve over Purcell's head. The two players then swapped sides of the court.

Max Purcell, *left*, plays a backhand volley in front of his partner, Matthew Ebden, during the 2022 Wimbledon men's doubles final.

Ebden also charged the net right away. By the time the ball came back to them, both players were standing in the two service boxes.

The return came high to Ebden's side. He attacked it and hit a low ball right at the feet of Pavić, who was at the net. The Croatian was able to use his reflexes to dig out the ball. But the shot went right to Purcell, who hit a winner down the right side of the court.

Ebden and Purcell went on to win the set and the match. Though this was just one point in a long match, it showed just how to win in doubles tennis. To be the best, teams must communicate and attack.

ATTACKING THE NET

Martina Navratilova and Pam Shriver were an almost unbeatable doubles combination in the 1980s. The pair won 20 Grand Slam doubles titles. From 1983 to 1985, they won 109 matches in a row. To Shriver, the reason was simple: both players were great serve-and-volley players. Put them on the court together, and they could dominate at the net.

While getting to the net is a good strategy for singles players, it's crucial in doubles. With two players on the other side of the court, it's difficult to find a spot to hit a winner at the baseline. Most doubles points are won on volleys.

Pam Shriver, *left*, and Martina Navratilova hold up their trophies after winning the 1987 women's doubles tournament at the French Open.

Both teams start with at least one player back at the baseline. Usually the team that can get both players to the net first will win the point. Shriver said that's what made Navratilova such a great partner. While Shriver was able to play careful shots that kept the duo's opponents deep, Navratilova was always working hard to get forward.

SETTING UP

When Ebden and Purcell set up for their crucial point, they were using a common tactic called the I-formation. And while

us open series
BANQUE
NATIONALE
IZOD
MONTRÉAL
IZOD

both players line up right down the middle, the key is what happens next. By splitting in different directions when the ball is moving, their opponents have only a split second to see which player is going to which side.

Teams don't always use the I-formation. But it can be a useful idea for key points in a match. One of the best men's doubles teams of all time was made up of twin brothers Bob and Mike Bryan. They liked to use the I-formation to change the course of a match if the other team was on a roll. "It's good to use the I-formation when opponents are returning really well," Bob Bryan said. "It's a way to get their eye off the ball and create some indecision in their return game."

CONSTANT COMMUNICATION

Before each serve in a doubles match, the server's partner at the net is likely to hold one hand behind their back. That way they can let

Mike Bryan, *left*, serves out of the I-formation, hitting the ball over the head of his teammate and brother, Bob Bryan.

the server know which direction the serve should go. A point toward the middle of the court could mean a serve down the center line. Pointing the other way often means to serve wide. If an experienced player knows where the serve is going, they have a good chance of working out where the return will end up. Knowing that, they might be able to pounce on the return and quickly win a point.

Lefty, Righty

Many good doubles teams are a combination of one left-handed player and one right-handed player. That way each can play on each side of the court and cover the doubles alleys on their forehands. Martina Navratilova (left-handed) and Pam Shriver (right-handed) as well as Bob (left-handed) and Mike (right-handed) Bryan succeeded with this type of partnership.

That communication does not stop while the point is going on. Doubles teammates are constantly talking during the play. They do this to let each other know who should be attacking the ball. If both players go for the same shot, they are likely to cross each other up. Even if they do return the ball, there is a good chance both players will be out of position for the next shot.

Chemistry is also important for a doubles team. Doubles teams change often as players look for the right partner.

Teammates Neal Skupski, *left*, and Joe Salisbury talk strategy between points during a match in 2021.

That was never an issue for the Bryan brothers. The two had played together all their lives. As professionals they won a record 119 doubles titles. One opponent said the Bryan brothers almost never talked between points. They had played together so long that they didn't need to. But for most teams, talking through the plan is the only way to win a doubles match.

GLOSSARY

ace

A serve that cannot be returned, earning a point for the server.

backhand

A swing at the ball on the opposite side of the body as the player's dominant hand.

baseline

The line at each end of a tennis court.

break

In tennis, to win a game when the opponent is serving.

doubles

A tennis match played between two teams of two players.

drop shot

A shot played softly just over the net.

forehand

A swing at the ball on the same side of the body as the player's dominant hand.

ground strokes

Shots made in tennis by hitting a ball that has bounced off the ground.

lobs

High arcing shots usually played over an opponent's head.

ovation

Long applause by an audience, usually done while standing.

volley

Hitting the ball before it hits the ground.

winner

A shot that passes the opponent to secure a point.

MORE INFORMATION

Books

Hewson, Anthony K. *Serena Williams*. Minneapolis, MN: Abdo Publishing, 2023.

Powell, Garry. *Tennis Skills for Kids*. Tea Gardens, New South Wales, Australia: John Reed Books, 2022.

Price, Karen. *GOATs of Tennis*. Minneapolis, MN: Abdo Publishing, 2022.

Online Resources

Booklinks
NONFICTION NETWORK
FREE! ONLINE NONFICTION RESOURCES

To learn more about tennis strategies, please visit **abdobooklinks.com** or scan this QR code. These links are routinely monitored and updated to provide the most current information available.

INDEX

About the Author

David J. Clarke is a freelance sportswriter. Originally from Helena, Montana, he now lives in Savannah, Georgia, with his golden retriever, Gus.